SENSE & SENSIBILITY

Jane Austen

LEVEL 2

SCHOLASTIC

Adapted by: Rod Smith
Publisher: Jacquie Bloese
Editor: Fiona Davis
Cover design: Dawn Wilson
Designer: Dawn Wilson
Picture research: Pupak Navabpour, Osha Mason
Photo credits:
Cover and inside images: © 1995 Columbia Pictures Industries, Inc. All Rights Reserved.
Courtesy of Columbia Pictures.
Pages 62 & 63: Topham/Picturepoint; Wikipedia; Imperial War Museum/The Art Archive.
Pages 64 & 65: Hulton Archive/Getty Images; The Art Archive.
Pages 66 & 76: L Bradshaw/Mary Evans; Hulton Archive/Getty Images; Historical Pictures Archive/Corbis.

No part of this publication may be reproduced in whole or in part, or stored in a retrieval system, or transmitted in any form or by any means, electronic, mechanical, photocopying, recording or otherwise, without written permission of the publisher. For information regarding permission write to:

Mary Glasgow Magazines (Scholastic Ltd.)
Euston House
24 Eversholt Street
London NW1 IDB

© Scholastic Ltd. 2009

All rights reserved

Printed in Malaysia. Reprinted in 2010, 2014, 2016 and 2017

Contents

	Page
Sense and Sensibility	**4–61**
People and places	**4–5**
The language of Jane Austen's time	**6**
Introduction: The Dashwood Family	7
Chapter 1: Leaving Norland	9
Chapter 2: Barton	14
Chapter 3: Willoughby	16
Chapter 4: Bad news	21
Chapter 5: Edward's visit	26
Chapter 6: Lucy Steele	28
Chapter 7: London	33
Chapter 8: Willoughby's letter	37
Chapter 9: Colonel Brandon's past	40
Chapter 10: Mrs Ferrars	44
Chapter 11: Edward's promise	47
Chapter 12: Marianne in danger	51
Chapter 13: Willoughby's story	53
Chapter 14: Mrs Edward Ferrars	56
Chapter 15: Together	59
Fact Files	**62–67**
Jane Austen	62
Love or money?	64
The London season	66
Self-Study Activities	**68–72**
New Words	**inside back cover**

PEOPLE AND PLACES

MRS DASHWOOD has three daughters: Elinor, Marianne and Margaret. ▼

MARIANNE is sixteen. She thinks love and feelings are the most important things in life. ▼

ELINOR is nineteen and Mrs Dashwood's oldest daughter. She is kind and has good sense. ▼

▲ **MARGARET** is Mrs Dashwood's youngest daughter. She is thirteen years old.

SIR JOHN MIDDLETON is Mrs Dashwood's cousin.

MRS JENNINGS has two married daughters. Her favourite hobby is finding partners for her unmarried young friends.

LUCY STEELE and her sister, Anne, are from Devon. Lucy is pretty, and loves to talk, but she has a secret … .

JOHN DASHWOOD is the Dashwood girls' half-brother. He is married to Fanny.

EDWARD FERRARS ▶

is Fanny Dashwood's brother. He is a young man with a good future ahead of him. Fanny wants him to become rich. But Edward wants to be a clergyman*.

* A 'clergyman' works for the church.

◀ COLONEL BRANDON is a

quiet, serious man. He is a friend of Sir John Middleton and often visits him in Devon. He has a secret in his past.

WILLOUGHBY ▶

is a handsome young man from Combe Magna in Somerset. He has no fortune of his own.

◀ PLACES

NORLAND PARK in Sussex is the home of Mrs Dashwood and her three daughters.

BARTON PARK and **BARTON COTTAGE** are Sir John Middleton's country homes in Devon.

DELAFORD in Dorset is Colonel Brandon's family home.

The language of Jane Austen's time

Jane Austen wrote Sense and Sensibility *between 1795 and 1811. The English that people spoke and wrote at that time was a little different from modern English. Here are some of the differences that you will find when you read* Sense and Sensibility.

Jane Austen's language		modern English
cannot	=	*can't*
I cannot believe it!		*I can't believe it!*
do not	=	*don't*
Do not speak of it.		*Don't talk about it.*
Why do you not …?	=	*Why don't you …?*
Why do you not ask Marianne?		*Why don't you ask Marianne?*
Must we …?	=	*Do we have to …?*
Must we go to dinner this evening?		*Do we have to go to dinner this evening?*
a handsome man / woman	=	*a good-looking man / woman*
a drawing room	=	*a large sitting room for guests*

People only used first names for children, families and very good friends. So Lucy Steele uses Miss Dashwood *for Elinor.*

When Jane Austen started to write this book, she called it Elinor and Marianne. *Later she changed it to* Sense and Sensibility. *'Sensibility' means having deep, strong feelings. Marianne's feelings are the most important thing to her, but Elinor is different. She thinks about her feelings, and uses sense to find answers to her problems. So, Elinor is 'Sense' and Marianne is 'Sensibility'.*

SENSE & SENSIBILITY
INTRODUCTION
The Dashwood family

Old Mr Dashwood lived at Norland Park in Sussex. For many years, he lived there with his sister. Then his sister died. Old Mr Dashwood felt sad. He did not like living alone. Norland Park was a large estate* in the country and suitable for a large family. So he invited his brother's son, Henry, and his family to live with him. Henry Dashwood came with his wife and their three daughters – Elinor, Marianne and Margaret. They were soon very comfortable there. The family were kind and the old man was happy.

Henry had a son, John, from his first wife. As a young boy, John and old Mr Dashwood spent some happy times together. And the old man always remembered this. John only visited Norland sometimes, but he was still the old man's favourite.

After some years, old Mr Dashwood died. He left one thousand pounds to each of the three girls. Norland and the rest of his money went to Henry.

* An 'estate' is a large area of land with one or more buildings on it.

'But when Henry dies,' he wrote, 'everything will go to John.'

The following year, Henry became very ill. He knew he was going to die. He was worried about his wife and daughters. He only had ten thousand pounds to leave them.

Henry asked John to come and see him. John and his wife, Fanny, were rich. Henry asked John to look after his three daughters. John was a rather selfish man, but he was not unkind. He promised to help. He decided to give Elinor, Marianne and Margaret one thousand pounds each. But first, he had to tell Fanny.

CHAPTER 1
Leaving Norland

Very soon after Henry died, John and Fanny arrived at Norland with their young son. Mrs Dashwood could not stop them – John and Fanny were now the new owners. But she was angry. She and the girls were still very sad about Henry. They needed to be alone. Did John and Fanny have no feelings?

Mrs Dashwood wanted to leave Norland at once. Marianne felt the same.

'We were so happy in this house,' Marianne cried. 'But now I feel it is not my home anymore. I do not even want to speak to Fanny and John!'

'We must speak to them, Marianne,' Elinor said. 'John has been kind to us. We do not want to upset him.'

Elinor was only nineteen but her mother always listened to her. But Mrs Dashwood understood Marianne's strong feelings, too. She and Marianne were very similar. Mrs Dashwood put her arms around Marianne.

'Do not worry, dear,' she said. 'We will buy another place as fine as Norland.'

'Do not promise what we cannot pay for, mother,' said Elinor.

Margaret watched but said nothing. She was only thirteen but she was already very much like her mother.

★★★

Fanny did not agree with her husband's plan to help Mrs Dashwood and her daughters.

'A thousand pounds is too much,' she said.

'But I made a promise to my father,' John said. He now sounded unsure. He always listened to his wife. 'Perhaps you are right,' he continued, after a few moments. 'It is rather a lot. Do you think five hundred pounds is a fair offer?'

Fanny moved closer to her husband and smiled. 'Think of your own son, John. Your father was very ill when he spoke to you. Did you really understand him? I do not think he wanted you to help with money at all. He left them ten thousand pounds ... .'

'That is more than enough,' John said.

'I think he meant you to help your sisters. To find a new home perhaps,' Fanny continued, 'or a present of food sometimes.'

John Dashwood looked at his wife. 'Yes, Fanny,' he said. 'I believe you are right.'

***

At the end of that first month, Fanny's brother, Edward Ferrars, arrived. He was quiet, kind and very different from his sister. He liked to talk to Elinor and watch her drawing. They spent more and more time together.

Mrs Dashwood was pleased. For the first time, she stopped thinking about leaving Norland. She liked Edward very much. Could he and Elinor become engaged? As time went on, she became certain of it.

'In a few months, I believe Elinor and Edward will be married,' she told Marianne one day. 'You will then have a brother. Edward is a good man. I am sure your sister will be very happy.'

'Oh, mother,' Marianne cried. 'How are we going to live without her?'

'Do not worry, dear. They will not live far away and I am sure we will meet every day.'

But Marianne still looked sad.

'What is it, Marianne?' asked her mother. 'Do you not agree with your sister's choice?'

'I think Edward is a very nice man,' said Marianne. 'But he has no real taste. I do not think he listens when I play the piano. It is the same with Elinor's pictures. He appears to like them. But does he really understand that they are very good? And books, also. Last night he read to us. But there was no fire in his words. I could never be happy with a man like Edward. My husband must have the same tastes as myself.'

For a moment, she looked lost. 'But I do not think I will ever find him.'

Mrs Dashwood laughed. 'Oh, Marianne,' she said. 'You are still only sixteen. You have all the time in the world.'

***

That evening, Marianne spoke to Elinor about Edward. 'I am sorry that Edward has no taste for drawing,' she said.

'No, you are wrong, Marianne,' Elinor said. 'Edward is unsure of himself, that is all. I like him very much.'

'*Like* him?' laughed Marianne. 'You sound so cold, Elinor. Is that all you feel for Edward?'

'No, Marianne. I am being careful. I do not know for certain that Edward loves me. And it is not only about love.'

'What could be more important than love?'

'Oh, Marianne. You and mother think only of feelings. Edward is not free. I believe his mother is no different from Fanny. She is a difficult woman with great hopes for her son. She would not like him to marry someone like me. I have so little money of my own.'

Marianne was quiet. She and her mother were wrong about Edward and Elinor. Their future together was not certain. Why was love so difficult?

★★★

Fanny was unhappy about Edward and Elinor. Fanny and her mother had great plans for Edward. Above all, Fanny wanted him to marry well.

'But, of course,' Fanny told Mrs Dashwood one day, 'Edward has not met anyone good enough for him yet.'

Mrs Dashwood was very angry with Fanny. 'We must leave Norland at once,' she thought.

Happily for Mrs Dashwood, a letter arrived for her the next day. It was from her cousin, Sir John Middleton. Sir John was writing from Barton Park, his estate in Devon. In the letter, he offered Mrs Dashwood and her daughters a small house on the estate.

Mrs Dashwood showed the letter to her daughters and

they agreed to move. The house was inexpensive. It was also far from Norland. But Elinor felt sad about leaving Edward.

At dinner that evening, Mrs Dashwood told Fanny and Edward the news. Edward looked very worried.

'Are you going so far?' he asked.

'My dear Edward,' Mrs Dashwood answered, 'you will always be welcome at our house.'

At the end of the week, the family left Norland. John did not keep his promise to his father. Mrs Dashwood now lost all hope of receiving any money from him. She and her daughters looked back at their old home one last time. They wanted to escape Fanny, but they also remembered happier times.

'Dear Norland,' said Marianne, sadly. 'Who will love you now?'

CHAPTER 2
Barton

The family were sad as they travelled to their new home. But when they reached Devon, they began to feel better. The country around Barton Park was very beautiful. The house, Barton Cottage, was so much smaller than Norland. But it was very comfortable and they all wanted to like it.

The next day, Sir John invited them all for dinner. He was a kind, friendly man of around forty. His wife, Lady Middleton, was rather cold.

Two other guests were at dinner that evening. The first was Mrs Jennings, Lady Middleton's mother. She was rather large and talked a lot. She especially enjoyed telling jokes about lovers and husbands. Both her daughters were married, and now she had only one goal in life – to find husbands for everyone else.

The second guest was Colonel Brandon, a friend of Sir John. He was a quiet, serious man, a little over thirty-five and unmarried. Both Marianne and Margaret thought thirty-five was too old to get married.

After dinner, Marianne played the piano. She sang beautifully. Sir John talked loudly during the songs. Colonel Brandon sat very still and listened carefully.

'It is clear,' thought Marianne, 'that only the Colonel knows about music.'

***

'I am quite sure that Colonel Brandon is in love with Marianne,' said Mrs Jennings, the next day. 'They will make a good couple. He is rich and she is handsome.'

The news soon reached Marianne. 'Mrs Jennings cannot be serious,' she said to her mother. 'Colonel Brandon is more than twice my age. It is unfair to make fun of the Colonel. He is old and not very well.'

'Not very well?' said Elinor. 'Why do you say that?'

'He complained of rheumatism* yesterday,' Marianne answered.

'I was not surprised,' said Elinor. 'Yesterday was cold and wet, do you not remember?'

'I am not saying that the Colonel is about to die,' Marianne continued. 'He could live another twenty years. But thirty-five is too old to marry.'

'Oh, Marianne, you are so sure about everything,' said Elinor, and left the room.

Marianne turned to her mother. 'Perhaps Elinor is right,' she said, 'and the Colonel is not ill. But I am worried about Edward. He has not come to see us. I believe *he* must be ill.'

Mrs Dashwood thought for a moment. 'Perhaps he is not yet ready to come,' she said. 'Was Elinor hoping for a visit before now?'

'Of course! But Elinor and Edward were so strange on our last day at Norland. They spent hardly any time together. And *I* cried more than Elinor! Why does she not show her feelings?'

---

* Many older people go to the doctor with 'rheumatism'.

CHAPTER 3
Willoughby

'I believe nothing in the world can be better than this,' Marianne said.

Margaret agreed. They both enjoyed long walks. They were walking up the side of a hill near the house. The sky was clear.

But twenty minutes later, it was dark with clouds. It started to rain heavily. They turned back and began running down the hill towards Barton Cottage. Suddenly, Marianne fell and hurt her foot.

A man with a gun and two dogs was passing by. He put down the gun and ran to help. Marianne was unable to stand. The man took her in his arms and carried her back to her home.

Elinor and her mother stood up, surprised. 'Please excuse me, madam*,' the man said. 'Your daughter has had an accident, but I am sure it is nothing serious.'

Mrs Dashwood liked the young man at once. He was very handsome and his manner was kind and polite. She thanked him and asked his name.

'Willoughby, madam. I am staying at Allenham, a house quite near here.' He looked down at Marianne and smiled. Her face turned red. Willoughby looked back at Mrs Dashwood. 'I hope Miss Dashwood will be better soon. Perhaps you will allow me to call again tomorrow?'

'You will be most welcome,' she said.

Marianne was very excited. When Sir John called, she asked about her rescuer. She discovered that he owned a small estate in Combe Magna, Somerset. He often came

---

* People sometimes use 'madam' for an older woman they have just met or do not know very well.

to Devon to visit his rich cousin, Mrs Smith, at Allenham. Mrs Smith planned to leave Willoughby her fortune when she died.

'I can see you will try to catch him, Marianne,' Sir John joked. 'He will make a good husband. But do not forget my friend, Colonel Brandon.'

Mrs Dashwood looked serious. 'My daughters do not spend their time 'catching' men, Sir John,' she said.

The next day, Willoughby called and the Dashwoods welcomed him warmly. He was soon deep in conversation with Marianne. It seemed they had the same tastes in music and books. And like Marianne, he also enjoyed dancing.

Soon, Willoughby came to Barton Cottage every day. He and Marianne spent a lot of time together. They talked and sang. Willoughby was Marianne's idea of a perfect man. He was young, intelligent and open.

When Marianne was better, she and Willoughby visited the Middletons and their guests at Barton Park. They talked together but did not speak much to the others.

To Mrs Dashwood, Willoughby was without fault. Elinor saw only one: like Marianne, he was too open with his opinions.

'The problem with Colonel Brandon,' she heard Willoughby say to her sister one day, 'is that everyone speaks well of him, but no one cares about him.'

'I think exactly the same,' cried Marianne.

'You are both being unfair,' said Elinor. 'The Colonel is not so uninteresting. He has spent many years abroad and has some wonderful stories to tell. He also has fine taste and good sense.'

'And he could not be more different from Willoughby,' Elinor thought, but said nothing.

***

It was now October. Dances began at Barton Park. Willoughby was Marianne's only partner. Marianne was very happy. In her eyes everything Willoughby did was right. Everything he said was clever. Her feelings were clear for everyone to see. But Marianne did not seem to worry about the opinions of other people.

Elinor was not so happy. She remembered her conversations with Edward at Norland. Here, only Colonel Brandon made interesting conversation, but he was not always easy to talk to. He only had eyes for Marianne. Elinor liked Colonel Brandon very much and felt sorry for him. She felt sure there was something sad in his past.

One evening at Barton Park, he sat watching as Marianne danced. Elinor sat next to him. He turned to her. 'Is it true?' he said. 'Your sister believes a person can love only once in their life.'

'Yes, but I do not understand her reasons. Her father was married twice. Perhaps she will change her ideas over time.'

'Not too much, I hope,' said the Colonel. He looked down, sadly. 'I once knew a young woman like Marianne. She had the same strong feelings and opinions. But then her life suddenly changed. It was not her fault. She had to learn the ways of the world. The result was … .'

The Colonel stopped. He did not want to say anymore.

★★★

'Willoughby has given me a wonderful present,' Marianne said happily, the next morning. 'It is a horse, Elinor! And you will be able to ride it, too.'

Elinor's mouth fell open.

'Surely you will not take this horse, Marianne. You have not known Willoughby very long.'

'I have not known Willoughby for a long time,' answered Marianne, 'but I know him very well.'

'But we cannot keep a horse, Marianne. They cost a lot of money.'

Marianne knew this was true. She couldn't keep Willoughby's present. She went to tell him.

'It is still yours,' Elinor heard him say. 'I will keep it for you. You will have it when you move into your future home.'

'Future home? Does this mean Willoughby and Marianne are engaged?' Elinor asked herself.

Later, Margaret saw Willoughby cut a lock* of Marianne's hair and put it in his pocket.

'I believe Marianne and Willoughby are engaged,' Margaret said. Elinor and her mother agreed.

---

* To give someone a 'lock' (or piece) of your hair is a sign of love.

CHAPTER 4
Bad news

At dinner at Barton Park that evening, Mrs Jennings asked Margaret the name of Elinor's 'young man'.

'I cannot tell, can I, Elinor?'

Everyone laughed, except Elinor.

'Oh please tell us, Margaret,' Mrs Jennings said.

Marianne felt sorry for Elinor. 'There is no 'young man', Margaret,' she said.

'Oh yes, there is,' Margaret answered. 'And his name begins with 'F'.'

Elinor was upset. 'Now Mrs Jennings will not rest until she knows who 'F' is,' she thought.

Luckily, Lady Middleton changed the conversation. They all began to make plans for the following day. They decided to go to a place called Whitwell. The owner was someone of Colonel Brandon's family.

★★★

They all met for breakfast at Barton Park the next day. But as they were leaving, a letter arrived for the Colonel. He looked very serious and left the room.

When he came back, he addressed Lady Middleton. 'I am terribly sorry, madam,' he said. 'I must leave suddenly on important business. I cannot travel to Whitwell. Also, your entrance will not be possible without me.'

This was unwelcome news for everybody. 'But we must go to Whitwell,' said Sir John. 'Surely your business can wait until tomorrow?'

'I am sorry,' said the Colonel. 'But *this* business cannot wait.'

As the Colonel rode off, Mrs Jennings turned to Elinor.

'I can guess the Colonel's business,' she said, softly.

'You can?' Elinor answered.

'It is about Miss Williams.'

'And who is Miss Williams?'

'Miss Williams is his daughter,' she said.

'Come, everyone,' said Sir John. 'We cannot be unhappy. We will take a drive in the country.'

Everyone agreed. Willoughby and Marianne left the others. They were away all morning and arrived back a long time after the rest of the party.

∗∗∗

At dinner that evening, Mrs Jennings turned to Marianne and said, 'You and Willoughby cannot trick me. I can guess where you went.'

'Where?' said Marianne.

'To your new house. And I hope you will like it.'

Mrs Jennings meant Allenham. Marianne turned red and looked away.

Later, Elinor asked Marianne about the visit.

'Why must I not go to Willoughby's house?' said Marianne.

'It is not Willoughby's house. It is Mrs Smith's house and she did not invite you. You went there alone with Willoughby. That is not right. And now you have allowed Mrs Jennings to joke about it.'

'I do not care for Mrs Jennings' opinion,' said Marianne, quickly. Then she went quiet. 'Perhaps you are right,' she said, finally. 'But, Elinor, it is a beautiful house.'

∗∗∗

Willoughby spent a lot of time at Barton Cottage. He was almost never at Allenham. They all thought of him as a son and brother already. He and Marianne seemed very happy.

'It is so strange,' thought Elinor, 'that he and my sister have not told us of their engagement. They are usually so open about everything.'

One morning all the Dashwoods, except Marianne, went to Barton Park.

When they came back, Willoughby's carriage was standing outside. As they walked through the front door, Marianne ran past them and up the stairs. She was crying.

They hurried into the drawing room and saw Willoughby. He was looking very serious.

'What is wrong with Marianne?' Mrs Dashwood asked. 'Is she ill?'

Willoughby looked uncomfortable. 'I hope not,' he said. 'But we are both rather sad. This morning, my cousin, Mrs Smith, gave me an instruction. I must go to London on business.'

'I am sorry,' said Mrs Dashwood. 'But I understand. When must you leave?'

'Almost this moment.'

'But you will not be away too long, I hope?'

'I will not be back for at least twelve months.'

'*Twelve* months? But you will come back and stay with us sometimes.'

Willoughby looked at the floor. 'I do not know. I will be very busy … .'

He stopped. Mrs Dashwood and her daughters were too surprised to speak.

'I can stay no longer,' Willoughby cried and almost ran out of the house.

★★★

'I feel sorry for Willoughby,' Mrs Dashwood told Elinor later. 'I believe Mrs Smith's 'business in London' is just an excuse. She wants to stop Willoughby from seeing Marianne. Willoughby has to agree because he has no money of his own.'

'I do not think this explains his strange manner,' Elinor said. 'He seemed a different man. I think something more has happened.'

'Oh, Elinor,' said her mother. 'How can you think badly of Willoughby? I am certain of his love for Marianne, and I am sure they will be married.'

'I, too, am certain of his love,' cried Elinor. 'But I am not certain of their engagement.'

★★★

Marianne was very upset now that Willoughby was gone. She didn't eat or sleep very much. She only read the books that Willoughby liked, and only sang the songs they sang together. She often went for walks alone.

In the next few days, there was no more news from Willoughby.

'He cannot write,' said Mrs Dashwood. 'Sir John brings us the letters. He could discover their secret.'

'That is true,' Elinor said. 'But why do you not ask Marianne if they are engaged?'

'Oh, I do not want to upset her with my questions,' her mother answered.

CHAPTER 5
Edward's visit

One day, Marianne finally agreed to join her sisters in a walk. They reached an area of open country. A long road lay before them. At its far end, a horse and rider appeared.

'It is Willoughby,' cried Marianne.

But it was not Willoughby. It was Edward. Marianne was disappointed, but she was also happy for Elinor. They welcomed Edward warmly.

'Have you come from London, Edward?' asked Marianne.

'Uh, no,' Edward answered. 'I have been in Devon for two weeks.'

'Two weeks?' Marianne asked, surprised.

'I was staying with friends near Plymouth,' Edward continued, quickly. During the walk to Barton Cottage, he seemed troubled and answered their questions with little interest.

Mrs Dashwood's welcome was also warm. For a few moments, Edward seemed happier.

The conversation turned to his future. 'What are Mrs Ferrars' plans for you now?' Mrs Dashwood asked.

'They are no different. She would like me to be rich and important. I am more interested in being happy. I prefer the church. But this does not please my mother.'

'You are right,' said Marianne, excitedly. 'Happiness is more important.'

Edward turned to Elinor. 'I see that your sister has not changed at all.' He looked back at Marianne. 'Nobody can love more than once in their life. You told me this – do you still believe it?'

'Of course.'

'You are right, Edward,' said Elinor. 'She has not changed.'

'She is a little more serious,' said Edward.

'You cannot complain of that,' said Marianne. 'I have never seen you more serious.'

Marianne was right. Edward's manner was strange. Elinor was uncertain of his feelings towards her. One moment he gave her warm looks, but the next he spoke coldly.

One afternoon, as he took a cup of tea from Mrs Dashwood, Marianne saw a ring on his finger. There was a lock of hair inside.

'I never saw you wear a ring before, Edward,' she said. 'Is that Fanny's hair? I remember she promised to give you some. But I thought her hair was darker.'

Edward turned red. 'Uh, yes,' he answered, uncomfortably. 'It is my sister's hair. It just looks a little different in this light.'

Edward stayed for a week. His manner towards Elinor grew no better. Elinor was disappointed. Sometimes she felt cross. But she decided it was because of Mrs Ferrars and her plans. Edward wasn't happy.

Edward was sad to leave Barton Cottage. He could go back to either Norland or London, but he did not want to go to either. Elinor was also sad when he left. But unlike Marianne, she did not want to be alone. Instead she kept very busy. To Marianne, Elinor's manner was as strange as Edward's.

CHAPTER 6
Lucy Steele

Mrs Jennings' other daughter, Charlotte Palmer, was now visiting Barton Park with her husband. Sir John invited the Dashwoods for dinner. Like her mother, Charlotte had a happy manner and always had a lot to say. Elinor discovered that the Palmers lived in Somerset. They were only a few miles from Willoughby's estate in Combe Magna.

'Do you know Mr Willoughby well?' she asked.

'Oh yes,' Charlotte answered. 'He is not at Combe very much, but I see him in London.' She moved closer to Elinor and said quietly, 'I know why you ask. Your sister and he will get married.'

Elinor did not answer. 'Do people in Somerset have a good opinion of Mr Willoughby?' she asked.

'Oh yes, nobody is liked more. Your sister is very lucky. He is lucky, too, of course,' Charlotte continued, quickly. 'Marianne is very handsome.'

Charlotte's information about Willoughby was not very useful. But at least it was not bad.

As soon as the Palmers went back to Somerset, two new guests arrived. They were sisters, and cousins of Mrs Jennings. Their names were Anne and Lucy Steele. Sir John invited Elinor and Marianne to Barton Park to meet them. Marianne was not pleased.

'Must we go to dinner every time Sir John has visitors?' she complained.

They found Anne boring. Lucy – the younger sister – was prettier and cleverer, but thought only of herself. It seemed the sisters knew everything about Elinor and Marianne already.

'I hear your sister has met a fine young man,' Anne said to Elinor. 'They will be married, I understand. I hope *you* will have luck soon. Perhaps you have met someone already?'

'Now the conversation will turn to Edward,' Elinor thought. She did not welcome this. The letter 'F' was now a popular joke at Barton Park. She was sure the Steeles knew all about it.

'His name is Ferrars,' Sir John said.

'Ferrars!' cried Anne. 'Oh, but we know him well.'

'Anne!' Lucy cried. 'How can you say that? We have seen him at our uncle's, that is all.'

Elinor was surprised. Who was this uncle? How did Edward know the Steeles? Elinor was too polite to ask more. And for once, Mrs Jennings did not ask her usual questions. But Elinor soon found out everything.

Lucy offered to walk to Barton Cottage with Elinor. 'I know you will think this a strange question,' Lucy said as soon as they were alone. 'But do you know Mrs Ferrars?'

'No. Why do you ask?'

A strange smile crossed Lucy's face. 'I have not known you long, Miss Dashwood, but I need a friend. I have not met Mrs Ferrars, but I will soon know her very well. You see, I am very close to one of her sons … .' She stopped and looked down.

'Really?' said Elinor. 'Do you mean you are engaged to Mr Robert Ferrars?'

'No,' said Lucy, looking up quickly. 'Not to Robert, but to his older brother, Edward.'

'Edward?' thought Elinor. 'How is this possible?' At first, the information did not worry her. She could not believe it. Edward could not possibly be in love with a woman like Lucy.

'I see you are surprised,' Lucy continued. She watched Elinor closely. 'We have kept it a secret.'

'For how long?' Elinor asked. She didn't want to appear too interested.

'For four years. We first met during our visits to my uncle's school in Plymouth. Have you heard him talk of Mr Pratt?'

'Yes, I believe I have,' Elinor answered. She began to feel worried. Could this possibly be true?

'Anne and I saw Edward during our visits to my uncle's school,' Lucy continued. 'We became very close friends. Our engagement dates from the year after he left.' Again she gave Elinor a strange smile. 'I know you will keep this information to yourself.'

'Yes, I will,' said Elinor. 'But why have you chosen to tell *me*. I don't understand.'

'I know that Edward has a very high opinion of you and your family. He thinks of you almost as a sister. Anne also knows of the engagement, but she has no sense.'

'But do we really mean the same Mr Ferrars?' Elinor asked, still unable to believe Lucy's story.

'Yes, of course. Edward Ferrars. The brother of Fanny Dashwood of Norland Park.' She took a small picture out of her pocket. 'Here,' she said, showing it to Elinor. 'Is that not Edward Ferrars?'

It *was*. The news upset Elinor deeply.

'He visited me a short time ago,' Lucy continued. 'Before he left, I gave him a lock of my hair in a ring. Perhaps you saw it.'

'Yes, I did,' said Elinor, quietly. So Edward's story of the ring was a lie.

Elinor was very pleased to reach Barton Cottage. She said her goodbyes and quickly went in.

Left alone, Elinor thought about Lucy's story. At first, she felt angry towards Edward. Then she remembered their time together at Norland. Her sister, her mother and Fanny were all sure of his love for her. She started to feel sorry for him. Lucy was very pretty. At nineteen years of age, this was all Edward could want. But now, four years later, he did not love Lucy. He felt unable to break their engagement, because it was a promise. This was all that kept them together. Elinor was sure of it.

***

A few days later at Barton Park, Lucy was making a present for Lady Middleton's little girl. Elinor offered to help.

'Thank you for joining me,' said Lucy. 'I thought perhaps you did not want to be my friend.'

'Why did you think that?'

'Your manner was a little cold. I thought, perhaps, you were upset in some way.' Lucy looked quickly at Elinor.

'No, I was a little surprised, that is all. But I am happy to be your friend. It must be a difficult time for you.'

'Yes. Edward has little money of his own. It is not enough to live on. As you know, I also do not have much money. Mrs Ferrars will not agree to our engagement. We must perhaps wait many years to marry.'

'You mean until Mrs Ferrars dies? Surely it is better to tell her of your engagement now. She will, perhaps, be angry – she has different plans for Edward. But, in time, she will change, surely?'

'No, she won't change. She will give everything to Robert. But we have a plan,' Lucy continued, speaking more softly. 'Edward would like to join the church. After he becomes a clergyman, I am hoping someone will offer him a position. Then he will have enough money to marry. I was thinking of John Dashwood at Norland. Perhaps you could speak to him?'

'Surely Fanny Dashwood is a better choice than myself?'

'No. She agrees with her mother.' Lucy suddenly looked sad. 'Oh dear,' she continued, 'perhaps it is better to end our engagement. It brings Edward so much trouble.'
She turned to Elinor. 'What must we do? What is your opinion? Can you not tell me?'

Elinor turned red. 'Certainly not. You must do as you choose.'

'But I would like to hear your opinion,' said Lucy. 'I believe you have good sense.'

Elinor made no answer. She decided never to discuss Edward with Lucy again. Edward was tired of the engagement. She felt sure Lucy knew this. But Lucy was interested only in herself – and only she could break the engagement.

CHAPTER 7
London

Christmas came and went. At the end of December, Mrs Jennings invited Elinor and Marianne to London.

'You are very kind,' said Elinor. 'But we cannot leave our mother.'

'Then I will ask her myself!' said Sir John. 'I am sure Marianne would like to see our friend Willoughby again.'

Mrs Dashwood was very excited by the idea.

'It is good for my girls to know the ways of London,' Mrs Dashwood said. 'They will both enjoy it.'

✭✭✭

Mrs Jennings' house was in Berkeley Street. She gave Elinor and Marianne rooms on the first floor. As soon as she arrived, Marianne sent a letter to Willoughby.

From that moment on, she could not rest. She ate almost no dinner and listened to the sound of every carriage in the street. Suddenly, there was a knock at the door.

'It is Willoughby!' she cried and ran to the door.

But it was not Willoughby. It was Colonel Brandon instead. Elinor welcomed the Colonel, but Marianne was too upset to speak. She left the room at once. Colonel Brandon watched her go.

'Is your sister ill?' he asked, worried.

Elinor explained that Marianne was very tired and tried to excuse her impolite manner. The Colonel did not stay long. Marianne was the real reason for his visit.

✭✭✭

'It is such wonderful weather!' said Mrs Jennings at breakfast the next morning. 'But it could keep sportsmen like Sir John in the country. And I would like him in London as soon as possible.'

Marianne felt suddenly happy. Willoughby was also a sportsman. He was probably also in the country. She spent the next few days hoping for bad weather. During this time, Colonel Brandon called every day. He talked to Elinor, but his eyes were on Marianne.

***

At the end of that first week, Elinor, Marianne and Mrs Jennings went out for a drive. When they came back, Willoughby's card was on the table.

'Oh no!' cried Marianne. 'He has been here while we were out.'

'Do not worry,' said Elinor. 'He will call again tomorrow.'

But Willoughby did not call. The only letter that arrived was from the Middletons. They were now in London and were inviting everyone to a dance at their house in Conduit Street. Marianne did not want to go. In the end, she agreed. But, without Willoughby, the dancing was very boring.

In the carriage on the way home, Mrs Jennings turned to Marianne and said, 'Sir John invited Willoughby to the dance. But he never arrived.'

Marianne looked very hurt. Elinor was worried that she could become ill. The next morning, Marianne again wrote to Willoughby.

***

Four more days went by, with still no word from Willoughby. At the end of that time, Elinor and Marianne went to a large party in town with Lady Middleton.

Marianne no longer cared if she stayed in or went out. Parties held no interest for her, but evenings at home were just as bad.

When they arrived, the two sisters sat quietly together. Marianne was bored as usual. Elinor did not feel like talking and was looking around the room.

Suddenly, she saw Willoughby. He was standing only a few feet away and was talking to a young woman in fine clothes. At that moment, Marianne also saw him. She stood up – a happy smile on her face – and began to walk towards him. Elinor caught her arm.

'Let me go! I must speak to him,' Marianne cried.

'It is better to wait,' said Elinor. 'I think he has not seen you yet.'

Marianne did not want to wait. But Willoughby's back was to them, so she sat back down.

At last, Willoughby turned.

'Willoughby!' said Marianne, warmly. She stood up once again and held out her hand.

Willoughby did not take Marianne's hand or look at her. He spoke to Elinor instead.

'How is Mrs Dashwood, your mother?'

Elinor was too surprised to speak. Out of the corner of her eye, she could see Marianne. Her face was deep red.

'Willoughby, what does this mean?' Marianne cried. 'Have you not got my letters? Will you not take my hand?'

Willoughby took her hand but the touch lasted only a moment. 'I called at Berkeley Street last Tuesday,' he said. 'I was sorry that you were not in. I left a card. I hope you saw it.'

'But do you not have my letters?' cried Marianne. 'I do not understand your manner. There is some mistake, I am sure. Please tell me, Willoughby. What is happening?'

At first, Willoughby did not answer. He turned and caught the eye of the young woman he was with. Turning back, he said, 'Yes, I was pleased to get the information that you were in town.' His look was strange and cold. He turned, and joined his partner.

Marianne's face was now deadly white. Unable to stand, she dropped back into her chair. 'Go to him, Elinor,' she cried. 'Tell him I must speak to him at once. I cannot rest. There has been some terrible mistake.'

Elinor knew that the other guests were watching them. 'I cannot do that,' Elinor said. 'This is not the place, Marianne. We must wait – just until tomorrow. Please try not to upset yourself.'

For Marianne, this was impossible while Willoughby was there. But then he and the young woman left. Elinor told Lady Middleton that Marianne was not well. She agreed to take them home in her carriage.

CHAPTER 8
Willoughby's letter

Early next morning, a letter arrived for Marianne from Willoughby. She took it up to her room. Elinor followed a few minutes later. She found Marianne lying on her bed. She was crying and holding Willoughby's letter. Other letters lay on the bed around her. Marianne pushed Willoughby's letter into Elinor's hands. Elinor walked over to the window and read:

My dear Madam,

Thank you for your letter. I am sorry to discover that I upset you last night. I do not understand why, but I ask you to excuse me. I did not mean to upset you in any way. I will always feel happy when I remember my time with your family in Devon. I have the highest opinion of your family – and think of you always as the best of friends. I never meant for you to think more than this. You will understand that this is impossible. I am engaged to another. In a few weeks, we will be married. I am sending back your letters. I also send back the lock of hair you kindly gave me. I will always be,

Your friend,

John Willoughby

'What a cold, horrible letter,' Elinor thought. She went back to the bed and looked at the other letters. They were all from Marianne. Unlike Willoughby's letter, they were warm and full of hope.

Marianne looked up at her sister. 'I bring you nothing but trouble,' she said.

'I want so much to help you,' Elinor answered.

'You cannot. No one can. *You* are so happy. You can never understand how I feel.'

For Elinor, this was too much. 'You call me happy!' she cried. 'You have no idea! And how can you believe I am happy to see you like this?'

Marianne threw her arms around her sister.

'I am sorry, Elinor,' she cried. 'But I will never feel happy again.'

'You must try,' said Elinor. 'It is better to find out about Willoughby now rather than later.'

'What do you mean by 'later'? We were never engaged!'

'Never?'

'No, he is not as bad as you think.'

'But you wrote these letters!'

'Yes. Was that so wrong of me? I felt we were engaged.'

'I can believe it. Sadly, he did not feel the same.'

'No, Elinor. I am sure he did. Others have turned him against me.'

'Then do not allow them to see you like this. Try to appear happy. Do it for me, for our mother, for your friends.'

'I cannot stay in London. I must go back home tomorrow.'

'Tomorrow? That is impossible, Marianne. We cannot upset Mrs Jennings. She has been very kind.'

'Soon then,' said Marianne.

'Yes, Marianne – soon.'

✲✲✲

'It is all about money,' Mrs Jennings said when Elinor gave her the news. 'Miss Grey has it. Marianne does not.'

'Miss Grey?' asked Elinor. 'Is she the young woman Willoughby was with at the party?'

'Yes, Miss Sophia Grey.'

'And is she rich?'

'Very rich. Oh dear, Sir John will be very sad to hear of this.'

Elinor put a hand on Mrs Jennings' arm. 'Please ask Sir John and all our friends not to speak of Willoughby in front of Marianne.'

'Poor Marianne! Of course not, my dear. You have my promise.'

Elinor thanked her. Mrs Jennings' worry over Marianne was real. She was kind, caring and a good friend to them both.

CHAPTER 9
Colonel Brandon's past

The next morning, Elinor wrote to her mother with the sad news of Marianne and Willoughby. Marianne sat at the table. She looked white. There was a knock at the door downstairs. Marianne went to the window and looked down. 'It is Colonel Brandon. Are we never safe from him?'

'Do not be unkind, Marianne,' said Elinor, but Marianne was no longer there.

The Colonel came into the room.

'I am sorry to call so early,' he said. 'But I met Mrs Jennings in town and she gave me the news. I was hoping to speak to you – alone.'

'Of course,' said Elinor. 'Please take a seat.'

Colonel Brandon looked very serious. He sat down. 'You will remember,' he began, 'that I told you of a woman I once knew. And that she was like Marianne … .'

'I have not forgotten,' said Elinor.

'Her name was Eliza. She had no parents and came

under my father's care as a child. Eliza and I were friends from the start. I cannot remember a time when I did not love her. But when she was seventeen, my father wanted her to marry my brother. There was no love between them and Eliza was very unhappy. Some time later, she and I decided to run away together. My father discovered our plans. He was very angry and sent me away. Eliza had to stay with my brother. I had no money and could do nothing. I took a position abroad.'

The Colonel stopped for a moment and walked to the window.

'I heard later that Eliza and my brother were no longer together. I often thought about her. I knew she had little money when she left my brother. I wanted to come back to England. But I had to wait three years before I was free. After six months of looking, I finally found her. She was very ill and living in a terrible place. I knew she could not live long, so I placed her in a good home. I visited every day. I was with Eliza when she died.'

'That is terribly sad,' said Elinor, 'after your earlier hopes.'

'That is true,' the Colonel continued. 'But I could not think too much about the past. There was a little girl – her child – to care for. Her name was Eliza, too. Her child was not my brother's. I placed her in school and visited as a father. Three years ago, I took Eliza from school and placed her in the care of a good family. For two years, everything went well. But then, last February, Eliza went to Bath with a friend. Sometime during that day, she disappeared. She disappeared with a man.'

'It is not possible!' Elinor cried. 'Do you mean Willoughby?'

'Yes. A letter came for me from Eliza last October. It

arrived on the morning of our planned party to Whitwell. Willoughby was the girl's lover. They met in Bath and ran away together. She had his child. But Willoughby left her with no money, no friends, and no address. He promised to come back, but he never did.'

'This is beyond everything,' Elinor cried.

'Now his true character is before you,' said the Colonel. 'I could not tell you anything of this before. I could not come between him and Marianne. I hoped he could change.'

'I am sure Marianne will feel better when she knows all this,' said Elinor. 'She cannot excuse Willoughby. Where is Eliza now?'

'She and her child are in a comfortable place in the country.' The Colonel stood up. 'And now I must go. I am keeping you from your sister.'

***

Elinor was right. When she told Marianne the Colonel's story, Marianne stopped making excuses for Willoughby. She was no happier, but her manner towards the Colonel changed. She was a lot more friendly.

The girls received many long letters from Mrs Dashwood. She seemed almost as disappointed as Marianne. Like Elinor, she told Marianne to be strong. She also thought it was better for her to stay in London.

***

Early in February, Willoughby and Sophia Grey were married. They left town soon after. Elinor was pleased. Marianne could not now meet Willoughby by accident.

But the sisters had a different surprise meeting. In a shop in town they met their brother, John Dashwood. He and Fanny were staying in Harley Street.

The very next day, John came to visit his sisters. Colonel Brandon was also visiting. After staying for half an hour, John asked Elinor to take a walk with him.

As soon as they left the house, he started to ask her about Colonel Brandon.

'Is he a man of fortune?' John asked.

'I believe so. He has a fine estate.'

'I am pleased to hear it. He is an excellent man. Your future appears comfortable.'

Elinor turned to him in surprise. 'My future, brother? What do you mean?'

'He likes you. I am sure of it.'

'Perhaps, but I am sure he does not see me as his future wife.'

'You are wrong, Elinor. At present, he is not sure, perhaps. After all, your fortune is small. His friends may not agree. You must try to catch him, Elinor. We will all welcome it.' John moved closer. 'Both Fanny and her mother will be *very* pleased. Fanny, you know, cares very much for your future.'

Elinor smiled to herself. She knew that Fanny really cared about a suitable wife for Edward. 'Is Edward going to marry soon?' she asked.

'It is not yet certain. But the family think Miss Morton very suitable. She is the daughter of Lord* Morton, and very rich.'

Elinor smiled to herself. Fanny and Mrs Ferrars' choice of a wife was very different from Edward's. They were about to be horribly surprised.

---

* A 'lord' is a very rich or very important man.

CHAPTER 10
Mrs Ferrars

The Steele sisters were also now in London. They were staying with the Middletons. The Dashwoods, the Middletons and the Steeles all met for dinner in Harley Street the following week.

Elinor and Marianne arrived at the same time as Lucy and Anne.

'Do you not feel sorry for me, Miss Dashwood?' Lucy asked Elinor as they climbed the stairs together. 'Mrs Ferrars will be at dinner. In a moment, I will meet my future mother.'

'Or Miss Morton's,' Elinor thought, but said nothing. She was very interested in meeting Mrs Ferrars at last. Edward and Fanny had very different opinions of her.

Mrs Ferrars was a small, thin woman. She spoke little and gave Elinor unfriendly looks. Her manner towards the Steele sisters was warmer. Elinor found it all very funny. She pictured the look on Mrs Ferrars' face when Edward told them about Lucy. She was even less suitable than herself.

After dinner, John Dashwood handed Colonel Brandon two of Elinor's pictures.

'My eldest sister did these,' he said. 'I know you are a man of taste. I am sure they will please you.'

'Yes,' answered the Colonel. 'They are certainly very good.' After a few moments, he handed the pictures to Mrs Ferrars.

'Hmm,' she said. 'Very pretty.'

'They are rather like Miss Morton's pictures,' Fanny said.

'Yes,' answered her mother. 'But then, Miss Morton does *everything* well.'

'Who is Miss Morton?' Marianne cried, suddenly. 'Who knows or cares about her? We are speaking of Elinor.'

Mrs Ferrars was angry. 'Miss Morton is Lord Morton's daughter,' she answered, coldly.

The room went quiet. Colonel Brandon watched kindly as Marianne put her arm around her sister.

'Do not listen to them, Elinor,' Marianne said, softly. 'I do not want you to be unhappy.'

***

'My dear friend,' Lucy Steele said when she called on Elinor the next morning, 'I am so happy. Fanny and Mrs Ferrars were so warm towards me. Did you not see?'

'They were certainly not cold,' Elinor answered.

Lucy was not listening. 'They are both wonderful women,' she went on, 'and they liked me – I could tell.'

'This is a welcome sign,' said Elinor, 'if they know of your and Edward's plans ... .'

'Of course, they do not. But I am sure it will all end well.'

At that point, the door opened and Edward walked into the room. The conversation stopped and everyone looked surprised and uncomfortable. Edward looked as if he wanted to leave again.

Elinor was the first to speak. 'How nice to see you again, Edward,' she said. She took his hand. She felt Lucy's eyes on them. Edward seemed unable to speak, so Elinor talked for him.

'I will fetch Marianne,' she said. 'She will be so pleased to see you.' Then she left the room quickly to give Edward and Lucy time together. When she came back with her sister, Lucy was sitting with her hands together. Edward sat beside her. He still said nothing.

When Edward saw Marianne's thin, white face, he asked, 'Do you not like London, Marianne?'

'No, but please do not worry about me. Elinor is well. That is enough for us both.'

Moments later, Edward stood up to go. Lucy followed him out of the door.

CHAPTER 11
Edward's promise

'I would like to ask Elinor and Marianne to stay with us for a while,' John Dashwood told Fanny.

His wife smiled, thinly. 'I do not think that is possible,' she said. 'I wanted to ask the Steele girls to spend a few days with us. They are great favourites with our son.'

As usual, John agreed.

∗∗∗

'My dear Miss Dashwood,' cried Mrs Jennings, a few weeks later. She hurried into the drawing room. 'Have you heard the news?'

'No, madam,' Elinor answered. 'What is it?'

'Something very strange,' said Mrs Jennings. 'Charlotte's doctor, Mr Donovan, told me. John Dashwood asked him to come to Fanny.'

'Why? Is she ill?'

'Not ill, exactly,' said Mrs Jennings. She sat down in front of Elinor. 'As you know, my cousins – the Steeles – have been staying with the Dashwoods these past two weeks. This morning, Anne spoke to Fanny. Fanny's brother, Edward, and Lucy are engaged! Only Anne knew about it and she is not very good at keeping secrets. Fanny was terribly angry. She was so upset that your brother sent for Mr Donovan! She sent both my cousins away from the house. What will Edward say about this? Fanny was most unkind.'

The news was out. Elinor could not now keep the secret from Marianne. She found her upstairs.

'How long have you known about this?' Marianne asked in surprise.

'About four months.'

'Four months? I can hardly believe it. Why did you not tell me? I thought you were happy.'

'I wanted to tell you but I did not want to upset you anymore. You thought I was cold. I was just trying to hide my feelings.'

'You have been so strong,' said Marianne, gently.

'I believe Edward does not love Lucy Steele. This has helped me. He made her a promise. And he feels he must keep it.'

'Oh, Elinor, I hate myself! You have been so good to me. And all I do is cry and complain.'

Marianne threw her arms around her sister.

✶✶✶

John Dashwood brought them the second part of the story the following day.

'After what happened,' he said, 'Mrs Ferrars sent for Edward. She asked him to break his engagement to Lucy Steele. Edward did not agree, so she sent him from the house. All his fortune will now go to his brother, Robert.'

Elinor was very worried. She wanted to see Edward but no one knew where he was.

The only person with any news was Anne Steele.

'Edward is going to Oxford,' she told Elinor, when they met a few days later. 'He will soon become a clergyman. I hope it will not take them too far away.'

Anne's news meant that Edward was still keeping his promise to Lucy. But when could they be married? Not until Edward found a position. And a clergyman's pay was very little.

✶✶✶

One afternoon, Marianne and Elinor were having tea with Mrs Jennings and Colonel Brandon. When they finished, Elinor left the table to study a picture by the window.

The Colonel joined her. 'I have heard the unhappy news of your friend, Edward Ferrars,' he said. 'Our clergyman at Delaford is leaving very soon. I would like to help Edward. I will be very happy if he becomes Delaford's new clergyman.'

Elinor took the Colonel's hand and thanked him warmly.

***

Later that afternoon, Edward called to say goodbye before leaving for Oxford. When Elinor told him of the Colonel's offer, he was very surprised.

'I cannot believe it!' he said. 'This is very kind of Colonel Brandon.'

'Colonel Brandon is a good man. He does not believe your mother has been very fair. He wants to help.'

'I will go and thank him at once,' said Edward. He hurried away. For once, he looked happy.

'The next time I see you,' Elinor thought, 'you will be married to Lucy.'

***

News of the Colonel's kind offer soon reached the Dashwoods. John came to see Elinor.

'Edward is a very lucky man,' John said. 'But please do not speak of this to Fanny. The news has upset her. And Mrs Ferrars knows nothing of this. I believe it is best to keep it a secret.'

'But why?' asked Elinor. 'She has finished with her son, surely? She cannot be interested in anything that happens to him.'

'On the day Edward keeps his stupid promise to Lucy Steele, she will feel the same for him as always. She can never forget that he is her son.'

'She forgot when she threw him out of her house,' thought Elinor.

'We think now,' continued John, 'that Robert will marry Miss Morton.'

'Miss Morton has no choice of her own?' asked Elinor. 'Is there no difference to her between Edward and Robert?'

'Certainly not,' said John. 'They are both fine young men. Robert is the older brother – that is all.'

CHAPTER 12
Marianne in danger

It was nearly the end of March. There was now nothing to keep Elinor and Marianne in London. The Palmers also wanted to go back to their home in Somerset. Elinor and Marianne decided to take the offer of a ride with them. From there, it was just a day's ride back to Barton.

They travelled for two days. The Palmers' house was large with lovely gardens. Marianne knew they were only thirty miles from Combe Magna. She felt sad that she was so close to Willoughby's home. But she was pleased to be back in the country. She took long walks alone in the gardens. The grass in the gardens was sometimes long and wet. It did not seem to worry her.

One morning, Marianne woke feeling strange. It seemed she was catching a cold. The next day, Marianne felt ill and stayed in bed. Elinor stayed by the bed and looked after her. Colonel Brandon was now also in the house. He and Mrs Jennings were very worried.

'Marianne has not been well for a long time,' Mrs Jennings said, and she sent for the doctor.

'It is nothing serious,' the doctor said. 'A few days of rest and she will be better.'

But three days later, Marianne was no better. On the evening of the third day, she suddenly became a lot worse. She was very hot and cried out in her sleep. Elinor became very anxious. Mrs Jennings was already in bed, so Elinor hurried to find Colonel Brandon. They knew that Marianne's life was in danger. They sent a man to fetch the doctor. And at midnight, Colonel Brandon left to fetch Mrs Dashwood from Barton Cottage.

Elinor stayed by Marianne's bed. She waited anxiously for the doctor. He finally arrived at five o'clock. The doctor was disappointed to see the change in Marianne. Elinor cared for her sister as well as she could. But when the doctor returned a few hours later, Marianne was no better. Elinor was happy about only one thing – her sister was still with them.

But by the middle of the day, there were small signs that Marianne was getting better. The doctor called and this time he had good news. Marianne was out of danger. Elinor had never felt happier. She stayed by Marianne's bed until she went to sleep.

CHAPTER 13
Willoughby's story

The night was dark and stormy. As the clock sounded eight, Elinor thought she heard a noise. She went to the window. A carriage stood at the front door.

'The Colonel and my mother are here already,' she thought.

Elinor ran happily downstairs. She opened the drawing room door, and stopped.

A man stood in front of her. It was Willoughby. Surprised, Elinor turned quickly to leave.

'Please, Miss Dashwood, wait! I need to speak to you. Just ten minutes, no more.'

'No, Mr Willoughby,' she said. 'You can have no business with me.'

'My business is with you – and only you. Is your sister out of danger?' he asked.

'I believe she is.'

'I am very happy to hear it. I have driven from London. I am here to tell my story. I hope you will then think me more stupid than bad.'

Elinor sat down at a table. Willoughby took the opposite chair. 'When I first saw Marianne,' Willoughby continued, 'I thought she was beautiful. I wanted her to love me. But I was not serious about loving her.'

Elinor was angry. 'Mr Willoughby!' she cried. 'I do not want to hear your story at all.'

'But you must hear me,' he continued. 'As you know, my fortune was never large, but I spent like my rich friends. Soon I was borrowing money. I could not pay it back. Of course, when Mrs Smith dies, her fortune will be mine. But that could take many years. I had no choice – I could only marry a rich woman. Clearly, this could not be your sister.'

Willoughby stopped and looked down.

'But I did not know anything about love – until I met Marianne. I have spent the happiest hours of my life with her. I decided, in fact, to ask her to marry me. But then Mrs Smith found out about … well, I am sure Colonel Brandon has told you.'

'You mean Eliza? Yes, I have heard the whole terrible story.'

'Yes, but remember who told you. Did he explain the facts fairly? Eliza was not without fault.'

'She could not go to you for help.'

'I had no idea she needed me. And no idea that she did not have my address.'

'What did Mrs Smith say?'

'She asked me to marry Eliza. I could not do that. So I had to leave the house. That night I thought about Marianne. I loved her. But I was frightened of being poor. I knew I could win the love of Sophia. At the time, the choice was clear. So I went to see Marianne and left her unhappy. But she still had high hopes for us.'

Elinor began to feel a little sorry for Willoughby, but she still wanted him to leave.

'Is that everything?' she asked.

'Everything? Not at all,' cried the young man. 'Then, in London, Marianne's letters brought back all my feelings of love. I hated myself when I read them. But it was too late.

Miss Grey and I were already engaged. I tried not to see Marianne. I watched your house and left my card while you were out. But then, there was that party. I decided to appear as an uninterested friend. When I left, I took one last look at Marianne. Her sweet face was as white as a ghost.'

'But what about your letter, Mr Willoughby?'

'My letter?' Willoughby smiled, sadly. 'It was Sophia's.'

'But the writing was yours.'

'The words were hers. She saw Marianne's letter one morning and read it. Then she ordered me to write to Marianne and send back all her letters. Also the lock of hair she gave me. I had to agree – or lose a fortune.' Willoughby was quiet for a few moments. 'Do you hate me a little less?' he asked.

'You were very wrong,' said Elinor, 'and you have been selfish. Marianne has been very unhappy. And this is your fault. But I see that your heart is not all bad.'

'Will you tell Marianne that I always loved her?' Willoughby asked. 'And that she means more to me than ever?'

'I will tell her some of your story, Mr Willoughby. But you have made your choice. Marianne's future cannot include you.'

'Does it include … ?'

Elinor knew Willoughby meant Colonel Brandon. She gave no clear answer, and Willoughby left. She knew he was deeply unhappy.

CHAPTER 14
Mrs Edward Ferrars

An hour later, the sound of another carriage drew Elinor to the window. It was Colonel Brandon with her mother. They were both very happy that Marianne was out of danger. Mrs Dashwood went to see Marianne at once and sat with her all night.

Elinor did not speak to Marianne about Willoughby's visit. For now, his story could wait. But Mrs Dashwood's hopes for Marianne's future could not.

'At last we are alone, Elinor,' she said. 'And you do not know how happy I am for Marianne. Colonel Brandon loves her. He told me as we were travelling up from Barton. He is such a kind, caring man.'

'I have never questioned the Colonel's character,' said Elinor. 'But do you believe Marianne will find him suitable? You know her opinions on age, and love for a second time.'

'In time, I believe she will learn to love him. Oh, Elinor, Delaford is not so far from Barton. Perhaps we could find a suitable house there?'

'Oh dear,' Elinor thought. Delaford was Edward's new home, too.

★★★

Marianne grew better every day. Finally, she was well enough to travel. The Dashwoods said goodbye to Colonel Brandon and Mrs Jennings and began the drive home. Two days later, they were back at Barton Cottage.

★★★

One afternoon, Elinor and Marianne went walking together. Turning to Elinor, Marianne said, 'I feel very bad.

Not only about Willoughby, but about you.'

'Me?' Elinor asked, surprised.

'Yes. You have been a good sister to me, while I have thought only of myself. And I have been unkind to others.'

Elinor smiled and took her sister's hand as they walked up the hill.

'This is where I fell,' Marianne said, 'and first met Willoughby. It does not hurt so much now, but I would love to know his true feelings.'

Elinor could wait no longer, and told Willoughby's story to her sister. When she finished, Marianne said nothing. She spoke only two words as they walked back inside. 'Tell mother,' she said quietly, and went up to her room.

***

'Do you know, madam, that Mr Ferrars is married?'

It was Thomas, one of the workers on the estate. Mrs Dashwood looked up from the breakfast table. Marianne's mouth fell open. Elinor turned white.

'Who told you this?' Mrs Dashwood asked.

'No one, madam. I saw it myself. They were in a carriage in Exeter this morning. I saw the younger Miss Steele. She asked about you all. She seemed very happy.'

'Was Mr Ferrars in the carriage with her?'

'Yes, madam. Only he was looking the other way.'

Elinor felt suddenly alone. Edward and Lucy were married. That was now a fact. But she could not understand the hurry. Edward was not yet a clergyman and the position at Delaford was not ready.

Elinor went outside to think. At that moment she saw a man on horseback. He was riding towards Barton Cottage. At first, she thought it was the Colonel. But no – it was Edward.

'Has he come to give us the news?' she thought.

The family welcomed Edward, but he seemed no more comfortable than before.

'Is Mrs Ferrars in Devon?' Elinor asked, finally.

'Uh, no,' Edward said, surprised. 'My mother is in London.'

'I meant Mrs *Edward* Ferrars.'

Edward was quiet for a moment. 'I think you mean Mrs *Robert* Ferrars.'

Edward got up and walked to the window. 'My brother and Lucy Steele were married last week and are now in Devon.'

Elinor could sit still no longer. She was so happy she ran from the room. She could not stop crying. For once, Elinor could not hide her feelings.

CHAPTER 15
Together

Edward Ferrars was the happiest of men. He was free of his promise to Lucy. He was now engaged to his love, Elinor. And they both welcomed a future at Delaford.

He explained the strange story of Robert and Lucy's sudden engagement. 'My brother first met Lucy when my mother sent him to her. She wanted Robert to talk to Lucy. And tell her to free me from my promise. Lucy had her own plans. She knew Robert was a rich man. Robert also liked the idea of tricking me and his own mother. They did everything in secret. My mother only found out after they were married.'

'How did you find out?' Elinor asked.

Edward took a letter from his pocket and handed it to her.

Dear Sir,

I am certain I have lost your love, and so I am free to love another. I know I will be happy with your brother. I hope you will also be happy. We will still be good friends, I am sure. Your brother and I have just come back from the church. We are going to Devon, but I wanted to send you a few lines first.

Your friend,

Lucy Ferrars

'I don't think I have ever read a worse letter than this,' Elinor thought. She handed the letter back to Edward without a word.

★★★

Only one thing now worried Elinor: the problem of money. They did not have enough to live on. Elinor gave Edward the idea of writing to his mother. In the end, he agreed.

The result was better than they hoped. Again, Mrs Ferrars asked him to marry Miss Morton and her fortune. When she saw there was no point, she stopped. She agreed to his engagement to Elinor and took him back as her son. She gave them ten thousand pounds. It was far less than Robert received from her – he was clearly still her favourite. But Edward and Elinor were more than happy.

★★★

Edward and Elinor were married in the early autumn. Soon after, they moved to Delaford. Mrs Dashwood, Marianne and Margaret visited often. During their visits, Marianne spent more time with the Colonel. Marianne discovered he was a man of good taste and excellent character. Over time, she grew to love him.

When Marianne was nineteen, she and the Colonel were married. Marianne's earlier opinions on age and second love were in the past. She was now the wife of an important man and she had an estate to look after. She enjoyed her new life. Elinor was never far away and the two sisters could meet every day. In time, Edward and the Colonel also became close friends.

Mrs Dashwood visited often, but she did not move to Delaford. She and Margaret stayed at Barton. Margaret now enjoyed dancing and was often at Barton Park. This pleased Mrs Jennings. Once again, she had a husband to find.

THE END

FACT FILE

Jane Austen

Jane Austen wrote her books in the 1800s. But they are even more popular today. What do we know about the writer behind the stories?

How many books did Jane write?

When Jane Austen was nineteen, she started writing her first book. She changed the story many times. More than fifteen years later, she finally published the story as *Sense and Sensibility*. She wrote five more books: *Pride and Prejudice*, *Mansfield Park*, *Emma*, *Persuasion*, and *Northanger Abbey*.

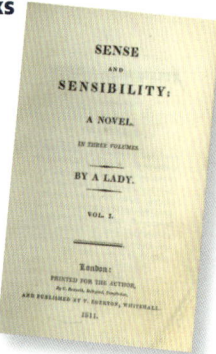

Who was Jane Austen?

Jane Austen was a writer from the south of England. She lived from 1775 to 1817. Jane came from a large family. She had six brothers and one sister. Her father was a clergyman. The family loved reading.

Was Jane Austen married?

No, but when she was twenty, she fell in love with a young man called Tom Lefroy. Tom, like Jane, had no money. He later went away to London. When Jane was older, a man called Harris Bigg-Wither asked her to marry him. At first, Jane said yes. But she was unsure, and she later said no.

Was Jane Austen famous?

Jane's stories were popular, but no one knew her name. Her name did not appear on her books. The publishers gave her name as 'a lady'. This was because writing was a job. In those days, respectable women did not have jobs.

Are Jane Austen's stories mainly for women?

No, not at all. More women read them, but men like them, too. King George IV loved Jane Austen's stories.

After the First World War, many British soldiers became ill because they could not forget the war. Doctors often told them to read Jane Austen's books. Her stories helped them get better.

> Who is the most popular writer in your country? What kind of stories do they write?

Did you know?

In 2003, the BBC did a survey to find the best-loved book in Britain. Three of Jane Austen's books were in the top 100.

SENSE & SENSIBILITY

Are Jane Austen's books still popular today?

Jane Austen died almost 200 years ago, but millions of readers from all over the world still love her books. Many of her stories have also become popular films. People of today are not so different from the people in Jane Austen's books. Women and men still fall in love with the wrong people. They still have problems with their families over love and money.

What do these words mean? You can use a dictionary.
publish / publisher   lady
respectable   war   soldier   survey

FACT FILE

LOVE or MONEY?

'It is all about money,' Mrs Jennings said. 'Miss Grey has it. Marianne does not.'

A marriage in the 1800s

For many people in Jane Austen's time, money was more important for a strong marriage than love. Respectable young ladies, like Elinor and Marianne in *Sense and Sensibility*, could not work outside the home. They needed to find a partner with money.

A rich partner

Edward Ferrars in *Sense and Sensibility* was engaged to Lucy Steele when he was a young man. But life as a poor clergyman's wife is not good enough for Lucy. So she marries Edward's brother, Robert, instead.

It was not only ladies who married for money. Willoughby also needs to find a rich wife. Willoughby was not careful with money. 'My fortune was never large,' he says, 'but I spent like my rich friends.' Jane Austen gives Willoughby two choices. He could be poor with a woman he loved. Or he could be rich with a woman he did not love. Willoughby loves Marianne but he does not marry her. He chooses money over love.

Did you know?

In Jane Austen's time, some things were surprisingly expensive.

	Now	1800s	
a woman's cotton dress:	$50 - $100	$350 - $400	
a journey of 80 km:	$3*	$185**	* in a small car in the US ** by horse and carriage

Unlucky in love

As a young man, Colonel Brandon lost Eliza to his brother. She later left his brother, but then had no money to live on. She met other men, but they did not stay with her. When Colonel Brandon found her, she had a child and was very ill. Sad stories like hers were a fact of life in Jane Austen's time.

Love not money

Elinor and Edward meet at the start of *Sense and Sensibility*. They fall in love, but Elinor has more sense than her sister. She knows that Edward's mother will not agree to the marriage because Elinor is not rich. She has only one thousand pounds from her father. When Elinor and Edward are married, they will have very little money to live on. They both know life will be difficult, but they choose love over money.

Secret engagements

Before young people married, they were engaged. An engagement was a promise to marry. Families usually welcomed an engagement that made good financial sense. But sometimes, young people wanted to marry only for love. They knew their families could say no. So they became engaged in secret.

'Sad stories were a fact of life...'

"The enjoyment of Elinor's company"
Chapter XLIX

There are a number of marriages in *Sense & Sensibility*. Which marriages do you think will be happy or unhappy?

What do these words mean? You can use a dictionary.
marriage   respectable   lady / ladies   cotton   journey   financial

FACT FILE

The London

In *Sense and Sensibility*, Elinor and Marianne go to London for the 'season'. What was the 'London season', and what happened there?

An exciting time of year

From January to June, young people came to London with their families for the 'season'. There were dances (called 'balls'), parties, breakfasts, lunches and dinners. It was the best time for young people to become engaged.

What's on?

A newspaper called *The Morning Post* gave information every day about balls and parties.

'Will you marry me?'

From the right young man, a marriage proposal was welcome. From the wrong person, it could mean danger. After marriage, it was almost impossible for a woman to escape a bad choice.

Most young ladies chose quickly and were engaged by the end of their first season. It was not surprising. In 6 months, the average young lady went to 50 balls, 60 parties and 30 dinners!

Out of time

Of course, not everyone found a husband. Some young ladies came away every year with no marriage proposal. As each year passed, it became more and more difficult for them. In Jane Austen's time, it was not usual to get married after the age of 25.

> What were the good and bad things about the London season for a young lady?

Season

The diary of Miss Henrietta Horrocks

Saturday, 5th February, 1814
4 p.m.

This morning at 9 o'clock I went riding in Hyde Park with my brother and Mama. I saw Captain Palfrey. He smiled at me. I am sure he is going to the ball at Almack's tonight. I am so excited!

At 10 o'clock, I had breakfast with Mama. After breakfast, we went to the shops. Mama bought me a new green dress.

At 1 o'clock in the afternoon, I went visiting with Mama. We called at cousin Fanny's, and then went on to my aunt's in Chelsea. I can't remember anything anyone said – I am far too excited about the ball!

Sunday, 6th February, 1814
4 a.m.

This evening was wonderful! At 6 in the evening, Colonel James and his wife came for dinner. After dinner, I joined the ladies. The men played cards until 8.30. I could hear them as I got ready for the ball.

Around 10 o'clock, I arrived with my family at the ball. Almack's is my favourite place in London! I am sure my new dress was the most beautiful in the room. Captain Palfrey was there. We danced together until 3 a.m.

Now I must go to bed. I do not know if I will sleep. Captain Palfrey will visit us later today …

> **What do these words mean? You can use a dictionary.**
> season   marriage   proposal   lady / ladies   average

SELF-STUDY ACTIVITIES

INTRODUCTION – CHAPTER 3

Before you read
Use a dictionary for this section.

1 Complete the sentences with these words:
   engaged   fortune   polite   selfish   serious   similar   taste
   a) Marianne and Willoughby are very … . They like the same books, the same pictures and the same music.
   b) Her choice of books and music is very good. She has good   … .
   c) Colonel Brandon never smiles. He is a very … man.
   d) It is … to say 'thank you' when someone helps you.
   e) My cousin is … . She will be married soon.
   f) … people think only of themselves.
   g) He doesn't own a house or have very much money. He has no … .

2 Circle the best answer.
   a) 'She cried because she was upset.' Which of these does this show?
      feelings   sense   taste
   b) 'I will marry you.' Which word describes this sentence?
      an idea   **an opinion**   a promise
   c) 'He is kind and friendly.' Which of these does this show?
      manner   an opinion   sense

3 Look at 'People and Places' on pages 4–5. Answer the questions.
   a) Who is sixteen?
   b) Which two people have secrets?
   c) Who likes to find partners for her friends?
   d) Who is married to Edward's sister?
   e) Who has good sense?
   f) Who wants to work for the church?
   g) Where is Willoughby's home?
   h) Where does Sir John Middleton live?
   i) Who lives at Norland Park?

After you read
4 Answer these questions.
   a) Why does Mr Dashwood leave most of his money to John?

- b) Why does Fanny not agree with her husband's plan to help Mrs Dashwood and her daughters?
- c) How does Mrs Dashwood feel when John and Fanny arrive at Norland?
- d) Why is Elinor's future with Edward not certain?
- e) What does Sir John Middleton write in his letter to Mrs Dashwood?
- f) How do Elinor and Marianne feel when they leave Norland?

5 Who is speaking?
- a) ' I am quite sure that Colonel Brandon is in love with Marianne.'
- b) 'Thirty-five is too old to marry.'
- c) 'Why does she not show her feelings?'
- d) ' I hope Miss Dashwood will be better soon.'
- e) 'My daughters do not spend their time 'catching' men.'
- f) 'The problem with Colonel Brandon is that everyone speaks well of him, but no one cares about him.'
- g) 'I once knew a young woman like Marianne.'
- h) 'You have not known Willoughby very long.'
- i) 'I believe Marianne and Willoughby are engaged,'

6 What do you think?
Marianne is open about her feelings for Willoughby. Elinor is more careful when she talks about her feelings for Edward. Who is right?

7 Writing
Write a short love letter from Marianne to Willoughby.

CHAPTERS 4–7

Before you read
8 What do you think?
- a) Chapter 4 is called *Bad news*. What will the bad news be?
- b) Why has Edward not yet visited Elinor at Barton Cottage?

SELF-STUDY ACTIVITIES

9 Complete the sentences with these words.
   carriage   complained   disappointed   position   ring
   a) The girls travelled to Devon in John Dashwood's … .
   b) Mrs Jennings wore a gold … on her finger.
   c) Barton Cottage was rather small, but Mrs Dashwood never … .
   d) Mrs Dashwood was … that John did not keep his promise.
   e) Edward wants a … as a clergyman.

After you read

10 Are these sentences right or wrong?
   a) Mrs Smith invites Marianne to visit Allenham.
   b) Willoughby will stay in London for only a short time.
   c) Edward has changed his plans to work in the church.
   d) Lucy Steele is engaged to Edward.
   e) Willoughby invites Elinor and Marianne to London.
   f) Colonel Brandon is Elinor and Marianne's first visitor in London.
   g) Willoughby calls when Marianne is out.
   h) Marianne wrote to Willoughby twice.
   i) Willoughby is friendly to Marianne at the dance.

11 Think about these questions.
   a) Why do you think Edward is strange towards Elinor at Barton Cottage?
   b) Elinor believes that Edward doesn't love Lucy Steele. Do you think she is right?
   c) Mrs Dashwood believes Marianne and Willoughby are engaged. Do you think she is right?
   d) Elinor is surprised by Willoughby's manner at the dance. Why do you think he is like this?

12 Writing
   Marianne goes home to Berkeley Street after she sees Willoughby at the dance. What do you think she writes in her diary? Write her words.

CHAPTERS 8–11

Before you read

13 What do you think?
  a) What will happen between Marianne and Willoughby?
  b) Colonel Brandon tells Elinor he once knew a girl like Marianne. Who do you think she was? And what happened to her?

14 Complete the sentences with these words.
  character   excellent   suitable
  a) This writer is … . Her books are the best I've ever read.
  b) Mrs Jennings wants to find a … husband for Elinor.
  c) He left his wife with no money. He is a man of bad … .

After you read

15 Complete the sentences with the correct people.
  Colonel Brandon   Edward   Elinor   Eliza
  Lucy Steele   Robert   Miss Sophia Grey
  a) … was Willoughby's lover.
  b) … and Willoughby were married in February.
  c) John Dashwood thought Colonel Brandon could be a good husband for … .
  d) Fanny told … to leave her house.
  e) Mrs Ferrars asked … to break his engagement.
  f) Mrs Ferrars' fortune will go to her younger son, … .
  g) … offers Edward a position.

16 What do you think?
  a) Lucy Steele says, 'I am sure it will all end well.'
    What do you think will happen between her and Edward?
  b) John Dashwood says that Elinor's future 'appears comfortable'. Will she marry Colonel Brandon?
  c) Colonel Brandon says of Willoughby, 'Now his true character is before you.' What do you think of Willoughby?
  d) Marianne says to Elinor, ' I bring you nothing but trouble.' How are the two sisters different?

SELF-STUDY ACTIVITIES

17 Writing
Mrs Ferrars asks Edward to break his engagement. Write their conversation.

CHAPTERS 12–15

Before you read
18 What do you think?
   a) Chapter 12 is called *Marianne in danger*. What is the danger?
   b) In chapter 13, Willoughby tells his story. What will he say?

After you read
19 Put these events in the correct order.
   a) Colonel Brandon comes back with Mrs Dashwood.
   b) Marianne catches a cold.
   c) Willoughby visits Elinor.
   d) The Dashwoods go back to Barton Cottage.
   e) Colonel Brandon goes to fetch Mrs Dashwood.
   f) Marianne starts to get better.
   g) Elinor and Marianne leave London.

20 Choose the correct answer.
   a) Willoughby has borrowed / has got a lot of money.
   b) Willoughby loves / does not love Marianne.
   c) Willoughby / Sophia wrote the letter to Marianne.
   d) Willoughby is happy / unhappy with Sophia.
   e) Lucy Steele / Elinor marries Edward.
   f) Colonel Brandon marries Elinor / Marianne.
   g) Mrs Jennings wants to find a husband for Anne Steele / Margaret.

21 What do you think?
Who do you like in the story? Who do you not like? Who will be happy? Who do you feel sorry for?

22 Writing
Write a new ending to the story. Edward marries Lucy and Willoughby leaves Sophia. What happens to Elinor, Marianne and Colonel Brandon?